PHONICS
Workbook

LEVEL 4

Published in Moonstone
by Rupa Publications India Pvt. Ltd 2022
7/16, Ansari Road, Daryaganj
New Delhi 110002

Sales centres:
Allahabad Bengaluru Chennai
Hyderabad Jaipur Kathmandu
Kolkata Mumbai

Copyright © Rupa Publications India Pvt. Ltd 2022

The views and opinions expressed in this book are
the authors' own and the facts are as reported by them
which have been verified to the extent possible,
and the publishers are not in any way liable for the same.

All rights reserved.
No part of this publication may be reproduced, transmitted,
or stored in a retrieval system, in any form or by any means,
electronic, mechanical, photocopying, recording or otherwise,
without the prior permission of the publisher.

P-ISBN: 978-93-5520-640-4
E-ISBN: 978-93-5520-641-1

First impression 2022

10 9 8 7 6 5 4 3 2 1

The moral right of the authors has been asserted.

Printed in India
This book is sold subject to the condition that it shall not,
by way of trade or otherwise, be lent, resold, hired out, or otherwise
circulated, without the publisher's prior consent, in any form of binding
or cover other than that in which it is published.

Contents

Double Consonant Ff..............4

Double Consonant Ll..............6

Double Consonant Ss..............8

Digraph Ng 10

Learn More 12

Digraph Ph 14

Digraph Gh 16

Silent Letters Gn and Kn 18

Learn More 20

Digraph Mb with Silent B 22

Digraph Nk 24

Digraph Qu 26

Digraph Wr 28

Learn More 30

Digraph Ck 32

Silent E 34

The –ell Word Family 36

The –all Word Family 38

Learn More 40

Double Consonant Zz 42

R-Controlled Vowels 44

Hard C and Soft C 46

Hard G and Soft G 48

Double Consonant Ff

Read these words aloud. Can you hear the ff sound?

Toffee

Coffee

Huff

Officer

Waffle

Read and circle all the ff words in the poem.

Little Jeff

Little Jeff

Sat on a cliff

Eating muffins

And waffles and truffles.

Huffing and puffing,

Came a fluffy dog

He ate the muffins

And ran away

With the waffles and truffles.

Teaching Tips:

Ask the children to make the ff sound repeatedly and then name words with the sound in them.

Word Bank.

Puff	Snuff	Cuff	Buff	Gruff
Coffin	Differ	Tiff	Doff	Scoff
Office	Bluff	Buffet	Dandruff	Scuff

Look at the pictures and write their names in the given space.

Double Consonant Ll

Read these words aloud. Can you hear the ll sound?

Yell

Full

Grill

Drill

Wall

Read the poem and circle the words with the ll sound.

Will and the Hornbill

Silly little Will
Went up the hill.
He saw a hornbill,
So he stood very still.
When Will went downhill,
He met his friends at the mill,
Who were all very thrilled.
So once again, they went uphill,
To look at the hornbill.

Word Bank.

Mill	Smell	All
Call	Cell	Tell
Tall	Small	Quill
Sell	Spell	Pill

Choose the correct ll word to complete the sentences.

1. The boy rang the .... (bell/ball/bell)

2. The children were collecting .... on the beach. (sel/shells/shel)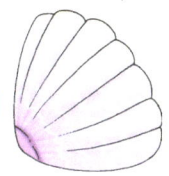

3. Jack and Jill went up the .... (hell/hill/hil)

4. Ted is my .... (dell/dol/doll)

5. The glass was .... of water. (ful/full/fulll)

6. My sister is short but my brother is very .... (tel/tall/toll)

Double Consonant Ss

Read these words aloud. Can you hear the ss sound?

Miss

Grass

Class

Tigress

Chess

Read the poem below and circle the ss words.

Missy and Cross

Missy has long tresses

She likes to wear pretty dresses.

She has a dog called Cross

Cross likes to eat candy floss.

Missy and Cross play all day

Under the sun and in the hay.

Teaching Tips:
Teach the children to say only one sound when consonant letters are doubled.

Word Bank.

Kiss	Mess	Less	Cross	Boss
Hiss	Moss	Fuss	Press	Princess
Pass	Glass	Gloss	Dress	Guess

Look at the picture clues and complete the words.

Dre..........

Cr..........

Che..........

Cla..........

Gla..........

Prince..........

Hi..........

Gra..........

Digraph Ng

Read these words aloud. Can you hear the ng sound?

Ring

King

Strong

Sing

Swing

Read the poem and circle all the ng words in the poem below.

The Nightingale

The young nightingale

Waved its long tail

It fluttered it wings

And sitting on a swing

It began to sing.

It sang all night long

Until everyone learnt its song.

Teaching Tips:

There are three possible sounds represented by the ng digraph. The first is the hard ng sound in *finger*. The second is the soft ng as in *challenge*, and the third, and most common is the ng digraph sound as in *sing*, *ring*, and *stinger*.

Word Bank.

King	Thing	Ring	Sang	Bang
Song	Wing	Young	String	Wrong
Hung	Ping-Pong	Long	Spring	Swing
Sting	Gang	Sling	Strong	Tong

Can you find the following words in the word search below?

king　　swing　　ring　　tong　　sing　　bring　　lung
bang　　wing　　sting　　bring　　thing　　long

s	w	i	n	g	x	u	z	f	x
u	y	w	x	t	q	s	b	l	e
q	g	s	g	h	t	i	r	o	u
b	e	t	b	i	s	n	i	n	w
r	m	i	a	n	c	g	n	g	i
i	u	n	n	g	w	d	g	h	n
n	o	g	g	m	t	e	t	s	g
g	r	i	n	g	z	a	o	q	r
e	b	h	k	i	n	g	n	r	v
o	j	l	u	n	g	u	g	g	q

Learn More

A. Sort the words given on the right into the correct category.

Ff Words	Ll Words
Puff	Hill
Stuff	Class
	Small
	Ill
	Wall

SS WORDS	Ng Words
Dress	Clung
Class	Tong
Grass	Thing
Press	Rang
Boss	

Words: Clung, Dress, Tong, Hill, Puff, Class, Thing, Grass, Stuff, Press, Small, Rang, Ill, Wall, Boss

B. **Look at the pictures and write the words.**

> stuff   dressed   off   smell

1. Do not .... so much food into your mouth.

2. Mummy .... up for the party.

3. Turn .... the lights.

4. There was a bad .... from the backyard.

C. **Connect the groups of letters to make meaningful ng words.**

Si		Sing
Ri		
Swi	ng	
Lu		
Wi		

Digraph Ph

Read these words aloud. Can you hear the ph sound?

Photo

Nephew

Aphid

Orphan

Dolphin

Read the poem and circle all the ph words in it.

Philip and Philomena

Philip was a pharaoh

His wife Philomena lived a life of sorrow.

So Philip brought a phoenix

Its neck was quite narrow.

One day a hunter hit it with an arrow

And it fell into a burrow.

Philomena moaned and groaned

Soon the Phoenix rose up in a glow.

Phew! Cried Philomena

And the castle was filled with her bellow.

Teaching Tips:

The digraph ph makes the same sound as the letter f. Emphasize the /ph/ sound often throughout the day. Make telephone the theme for the week. Let children read books about the invention of telephone.

Word Bank.

Dolphin	Elephant	Amphibian	Phantom	Pharmacy	Alphabet
Telephone	Graph	Phonic	Trophy	Phrase	Digraph

Complete the words by filling in the missing ph sound.

Dol …… …… in

Micro …… …… one

Nym …… ……

Am …… …… ibian

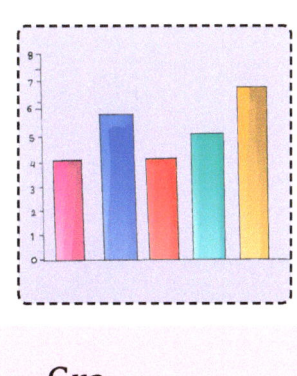

Gra …… ……

Tro …… …… y

Digraph Gh

Read these words aloud.

Ghost

Fright

Sleigh

Laugh

Neigh

Read and circle all the gh words in the poem below.

The Hag in Rags

Old hag Wright
Was such a sight.
Her hair was rough,
Her skin was tough.
She looked like a ghost,
But she loved pot roast.
Whoever saw her at night,
Ran away in a fright.
But old hag Wright,
Only sat and sighed.

Teaching Tips:

When gh comes at the beginning of a word, it has the sound /g/ (e.g., ghost). 2) When gh comes at the end of a word, it sometimes has the sound /f/ (e.g., laugh). 3) In most words, the gh is silent. When the vowel i comes before the gh, the i is long, and the gh is silent (e.g., high; night).

Word Bank.

Tight	Light	Rough
Dough	Cough	Through
High	Tough	Daughter
Weigh	Enough	Bright

Choose the correct gh word to complete the sentences given below.

| daughter | right | ghosts | caught | bright |
| laughter | knight | sight | night | through |

1. The boy .... the fish alive.

2. Mr Jones has a son and a ....

3. The brave .... fought the enemy.

4. I like watching stars at ....

5. I got all my answers ....

6. The sun is a .... star.

7. The train passed .... the tunnel.

8. A rainbow is a beautiful ....

9. .... is the best medicine.

10. Do you believe in .... ?

Silent Letters Gn and Kn

Read the words aloud. Can you hear the n sound in them?

Knight

Knife

Gnome

Knit

Gnu

Read and circle all the gn and kn words in the passage below.

Knoa and Gnana

Knoa and Gnana lived in a small village. Knoa had a gnu. Gnana loved to knit. She carried the yarn and the needles in a knapsack. Gnana knitted all day while Knoa and his friends played with the gnu.

Teaching Tips:
When kn and gn is sounded together, the k and g remain silent and n is sounded.

Word Bank.

Sign	Knee	Align
Gnarl	Knob	Design
Knave	Knock	Knowledge

Can you find the gn and kn words in the word search?

| knob | gnu | know | knock | gnome |
| long | kneel | knit | sign | design |

d	e	s	i	g	n	u
v	g	l	k	k	k	z
k	n	s	n	n	n	l
n	o	i	e	o	i	o
o	m	g	e	b	t	n
c	e	n	l	f	c	g
k	n	k	n	o	w	g

Learn More

A. Read and solve the riddles.

| Knob | Gnu | Phone | Knot | Trophy |
| Alphabets | Elephant | Night | Know | Gnaw |

1. Synonym for chew: ....
2. This is turned to open a door: ....
3. A mammal that lives in grasslands: ....
4. You use it to talk to your friends: ....
5. Something tied in a rope: ....
6. You win it as a prize: ....
7. A set of letters: ....
8. An animal with a big trunk: ....
9. The opposite of day: ....
10. A synonym for understand: ....

B. Read the sentence and write the word for the picture clue.

1. The boy fell and hurt his ....

2. Look for the road ....

3. A .... on the door.

5. The .... rode on the horse to the castle.

6. Grandma is .... a scarf for me.

C. Match the words or phrases in column A with the correct word in column B.

Column A	Column B
Body Part	Signature
Elf	Dolphin
Sea Mammal	Ignore
Uncle	Gnome
Autograph	Nephew
To Not Pay Attention	Knowledge
Books	Knee

D. Fill in the blanks with the correct word.

1. Sheryl is not from our country, she is a _____. (foreigner/forum)

2. I like the _____ on the scarf. (disease/design)

3. The king _____ for twenty years. (reigned/resigned)

4. Jimmy had no parents so he was an _____. (often/orphan)

5. We took several _____ of the pyramids. (phones/photos)

Digraph Mb with Silent B

Read the following words.

Bomb

Lamb

Comb

Thumb

Limb

Read the poem and circle the mb words in it.

Ned and the Bee

Ned and Ted climbed up a mango tree

There they saw a busy bee

The bee stung Ned's thumb

And he fell down with a thump.

Teaching Tips:

The sound b is silent in the mb combinations at the end of words as in comb and lamb.

Word Bank.

Numb	Number	Dumb
Bamboo	Jumble	Plumber
Crumb	Climb	Cucumber

Complete the words by filling in the missing mb sound.

Cru ....

Plu .... er

Ba .... oo

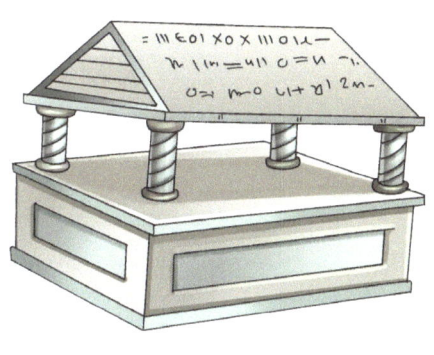

To ....

Cru ....

U .... rella

Digraph Nk

Read the following words. Can you hear the nk sound?

Ink

Drink

Sink

Monkey

Blanket

Read the poem and circle the nk words in it.

Naughty Frank

Naughty little Frank
Liked to play pranks.
He never drank his milk,
And poured it in the sink.
This made his mother angry,
And she made him stay hungry.

Teaching Tips:

The digraph nk makes the nk sound as in words like pink and sink.

Word Bank.

Ankle	Shrink	Frank	Junk
Blink	Sprinkle	Bank	Pink
Rink	Think	Tank	Plank

Read and Enjoy

Inky and Pinky

Inky and Pinky are two little monkeys. They live on a tree by the bank of a river. They swing from the branches of the tree. They are busy collecting nk words that are floating in the river.

Read the words in the river and write the ones which Inky and Pinky are collecting in the given space.

Digraph Qu

Read the following words. Can you hear the qu sound?

Quilt

Queen

Quiet

Question

Quail

Circle the words with qu in the poem below.

Quentin and Quinn

Quentin and Quinn were ready for the quiz. That morning, they got out of their quilts very excited. But on the way, Quentin and Quinn had quite a big quarrel. They go so late that they almost had to quit the quiz. When the quiz started, they were quivering with excitement. They quickly answered all the questions correctly while the others stayed quiet. Quentin and Quinn shared the quiz trophy.

Teaching Tips:

The sound qu is really two sounds: a/k and a/w. However <qu> we say kw together in order to hear a word.

Word Bank.

Quick	Aquarium	Quiz
Quack	Quarrel	Squash
Equal	Query	Liquid
Equator	Request	Earthquake

Complete the words by filling in the missing qu sound.

......iet

S......irrel

......ack

A......arium

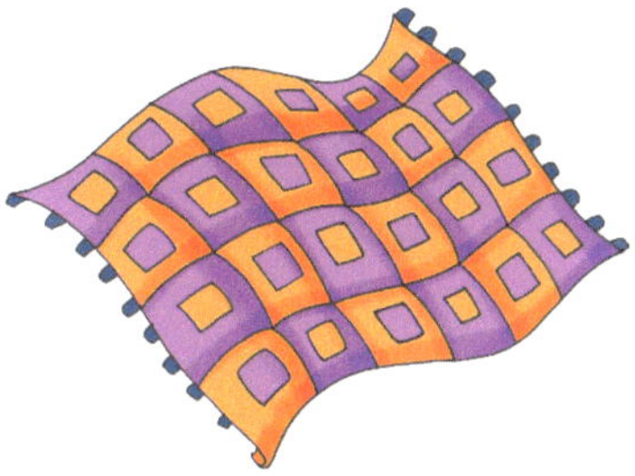

......ilt

......arrel

......ail

......estion

Digraph Wr

Read the following words. Can you hear the wr sound?

Wren

Wrist

Wreath

Wrapper

Wring

Read the passage and identify the wr words in it.

It was my grandma's seventieth birthday. I wrote a poem for her and made her a birthday card. I bought her a wristwatch and wrapped it in a beautiful paper.

My grandma has wrinkles on her face. But she is a strong lady and can wrestle with anyone. It would be wrong to say that she is weak.

Teaching Tips:

In the digraph wr, the w remains silent.

Word Bank.

Write	Wrinkle	Wrench	Wreck	Wrong
Wrap	Wrist	Wrestle	Wrath	Wriggle

Write a rhyming word beginning with wr for each word given below. The first one has been done for you.

Long	Wrong
Sprinkle	....
Kite	....
Cap	....
Neck	....
Twist	....
Bench	....
Vessel	....
Jiggle	....

Learn More

A. **Fill up the blanks with nk words.**

1. If you mix red and white you get _____ .

2. I use my brain to _____ .

3. I save my money in a _____ .

4. I like to go skating in the ice _____ .

5. A _____ likes to eat bananas.

6. _____ some salt and pepper on the salad.

B. **Fill in the blanks with the correct words.**

| bamboo | thumb | wrist | equal | request |
| wrap | crumbs | questions | wrong | square |

1. Can you _____ this gift for me?

2. You dropped some bread _____ on the table.

3. He would never accept that he is _____ .

4. Please answer all my _____ .

5. I hope you won't refuse my _____ .

6. Make sure you get an _____ share.

7. The mall is near the main _____ market.

8. She wore a gold bangle on her _____ .

9. The baby likes to suck her _____ .

10. That swing is made of _____ sticks.

C. Match the correct phrase with the correct wr, mb and wr words.

Column A	Column B
To be silent	Quick
A pen is used to do this	Wrong
To sleep	Write
To go up a tree or stairs	Quiet
The opposite of right	Climb
To be fast	Slumber

D. Match the related nk, mb, qu and wr words.

Column A	Column B
Quill	King
Monkey	Fall
Colouring	Ring
Tumble	Pink
Bangle	Climb
Queen	Ink

Digraph Ck

Read the following words. Can you hear the ck sound?

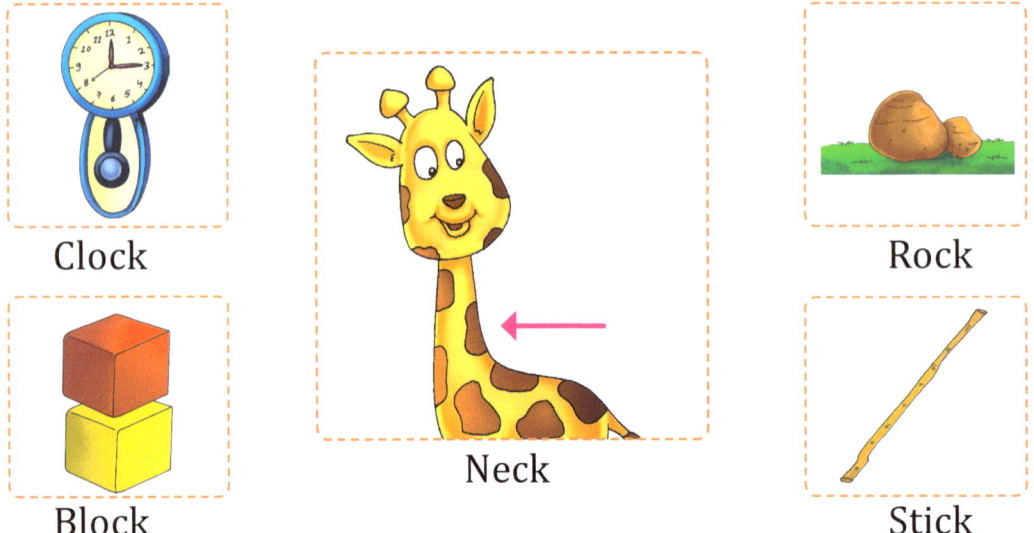

Clock

Block

Neck

Rock

Stick

Circle all the ck words in the story.

Ricky works at the zoo. He loves birds. Ducks are his favourite. He likes to hear them quack all day.
One day Ricky buys a new cuckoo clock. The cuckoo clock sings cluckcoo cluckcoo. He wonders if cuckoos coo or cluck and if clocks cluck or go tick tock.
Every morning when the clock sings, 'cluckcoo cluckcoo,' Ricky picks up his sack and straps it to his back. He puts on his socks and his shoes. He locks the door and heads to the zoo.

What is the name of the boy in the story?

....

What sounds do cuckoo clocks make?

....

What sounds do ducks make?

....

Teaching Tips:
Ask the children to snap their fingers and make a clicking sound.

Word Bank.

Sack	Cricket	Rocket	Tick	Black	Brick
Jacket	Duck	Bank	Pack	Truck	Lick
Sick	Pick	Luck	Peck	Frock	Chick

Look at the picture, blend the correct sounds and write the words.

(truck)	Tr Br | a u | ck kk	Truck
(clock)	Bl Cl | o oa | kk ck	....
(sick boy)	Z S | e i | ck kk	....
(black ink)	Bl B | a e | ck kk	....
(snack)	S Sn | ae a | kk ck	....
(tick)	T Cl | e i | kk ck	....
(frock)	Fr Ff | o oa | ck kk	....

33

Silent E

Read the words below.

Skateboard

Page

Pipe

Flute

Dove

Listen to the vowel sound in the word kit. Add an e, and say the word kite. Did the vowel sound change? The e at the end of kite makes the vowel say its name.

Look at the pictures below. Make magic by adding a silent e at the end of words on the right. The first one has been done for you.

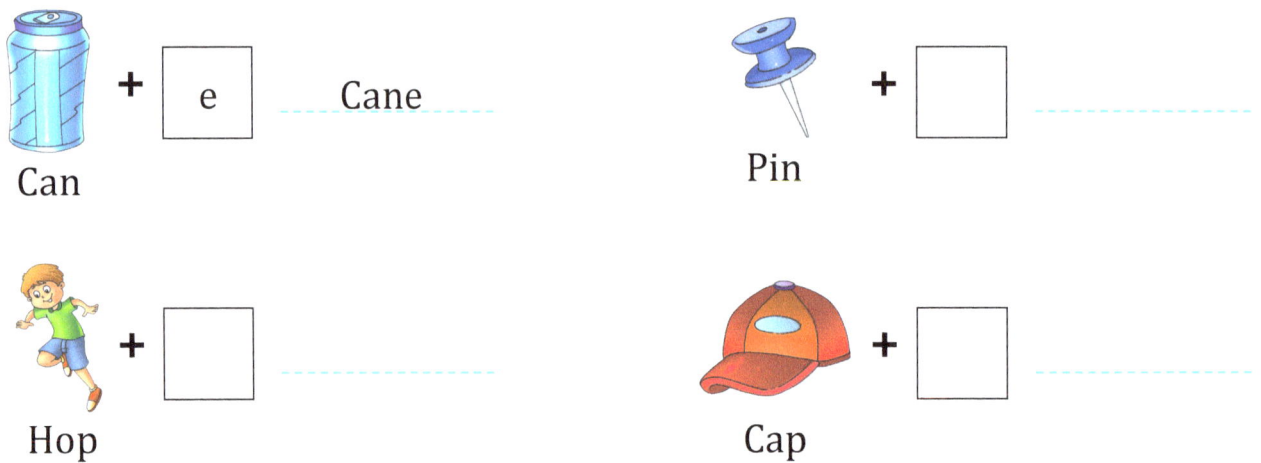

Can + e   Cane

Pin +

Hop +

Cap +

Teaching Tips:

A silent e changes the sound of the vowel that comes before it in to a long vowel sound. Help children understand the same with the help of the questions given above.

Word Bank.

Cape	Mane	Mile	Lame	Poke
Cute	Cube	Gate	Fate	Pale

Find the magic e words in the maze and help Jake reach his house.

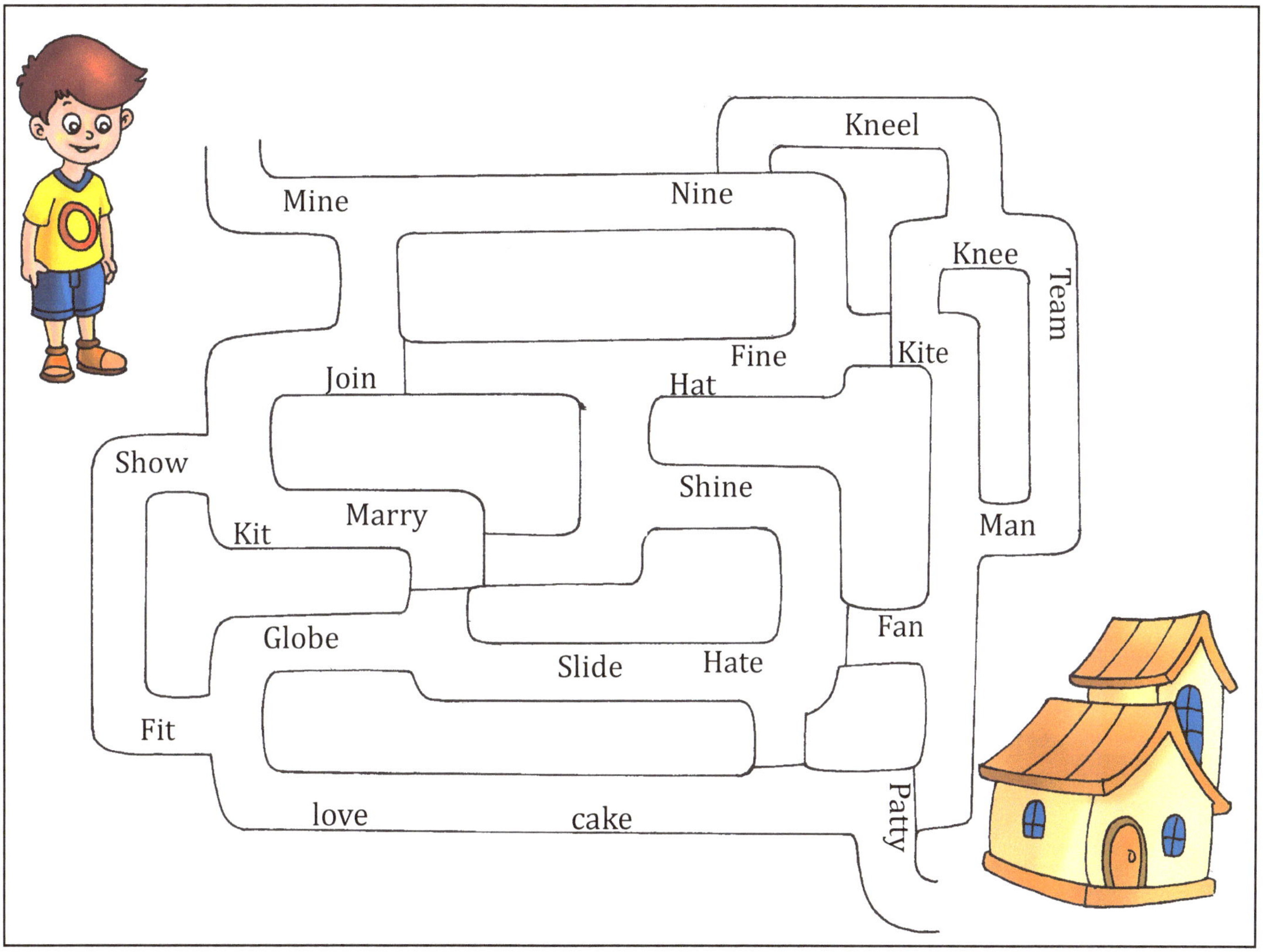

The –ell Word Family

Read the following words. Can you hear the -ell sound?

Well

Yell

Shell

Bell

Cell

Read the poem below and circle all the words that have –ell in them.

Stella's Stories

Stella was a famous storyteller,

She lived near the well in a cellar.

Kelly, Nelly and Shelley,

Rang Stella's doorbell.

They listened to the stories,

That Stella began to tell.

Stella's stories weaved a magic spell,

They forgot everything and asked her to retell.

Teaching Tips:
Add different consonants to –ell and make new words.
For example, f + ell = fell, s + ell = sell

Word Bank.

Tell	Sell	Nutshell	Fell	Smell	Dell
Dwell	Hell	Spell	Swell	Quell	Shell
Yellow	Bell	Yell	Retell	Well	Cell

Fill in the blanks using words from the –ell family.

1. Did you ring the door _____ ?

2. John is not feeling _____ .

3. Don't _____ at me.

4. The boy _____ down the stairs.

5. The foolish goat jumped into the _____ .

6. Do you want me to _____ you a story?

37

The –all Word Family

Read the following words. Can you hear the -all sound?

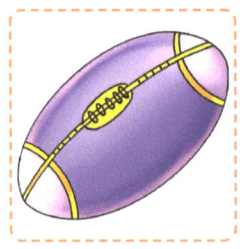
Ball

Tall

Fall

Wall

Small

Circle all the –all words in the poem below.

The Great Fall

Humpty Dumpty sat on a tall wall.

He was scared that now he would fall.

He wished that the wall were small.

Then Humpty Dumpty would never fall.

Teaching Tips:
Whenever –all is added to a consonant, the letter 'a' makes the aw sound.

Word Bank.

All	Call	Hall
Small	Thrall	Squall
Mall	Stall	Gall

Can you find the following –all words in the wordsearch below?

i	n	s	t	a	l	l	p	o
v	c	r	h	s	f	i	a	g
i	a	s	r	t	a	g	u	j
s	l	m	a	a	l	w	d	t
q	l	a	l	l	l	s	a	a
u	m	l	l	l	w	g	l	l
a	a	l	q	x	a	a	l	l
l	l	e	b	a	l	l	n	x
l	l	h	a	l	l	l	u	z

all
ball
call
fall
gall
hall
install
mall
small
squall
stall
tall
thrall
wall

Learn More

A. **Circle the correct word.**

   1. I think that puppy is cut/cute.
   2. Mother sent a not/note to my teacher.
   3. Put the toys in that tub/tube.
   4. The bucket fell/fel into the well/wel.
   5. Electricity can give us a shock/shok.
   6. Call/Cal me when you reach home.
   7. The sink/sank is in a mess.
   8. Let us bake/bak a cak/cake.

B. **Look at the newspaper and find 2 words each for the things that have the sound of ck, ell, all and words with the magic e. Write them below in the space provided.**

40

C. Match the magic e words with the correct ck, all, ell words.

Column A	Column B
Game	Ticket
Ride	Wall
Stone	Cricket
Time	Rock
Fence	Bell
Jingle	Clock

D. Fill in the blanks with the correct ck, ell, all and magic e words.

| frocks   track   shakes   horse   shells   smell   fall |

1. I love drinking mango ....

2. The market had a number of beautiful ....

3. Timmy fell off his ....

4. Humpty Dumpty had a great ....

5. We collected many sea .... at the beach.

6. There is a very bad .... around the garbage bin.

Double Consonant Zz

Read the following words. Can you hear the zz sound?

Pizza

Puzzle

Buzz

Fizz

Jazz

Read the poem below. Circle the words with zz sound in the poem.

Grizzle the Bee

Grizzle the bumblebee,

Flew from the gum tree.

Grizzle dazzled,

As it drizzled.

He buzzed inside a bus,

And made a fuss.

Grizzle had a lot of yellow fuzz,

It puzzled the people in the bus.

Teaching Tips:

Short words with short vowel sounds usually end with zz.

Word Bank.

Fuzz	Nozzle	Dazzle	Sizzle
Whizz	Jacuzzi	Frizz	Dizzy

Tick (✓) the correct word by looking at the picture clue.

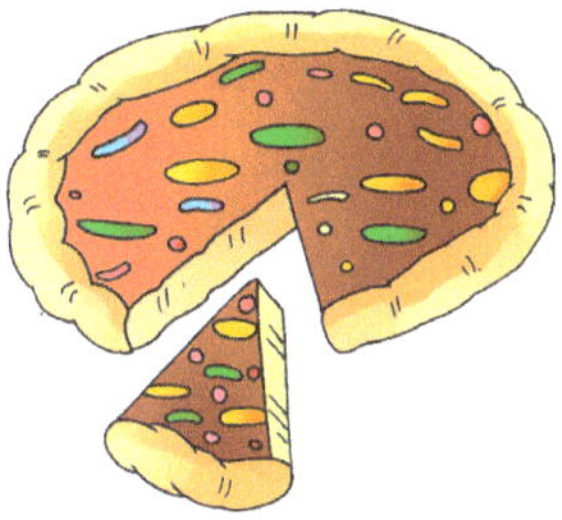

Pasta ☐ Cake ☐ Pizza ☐

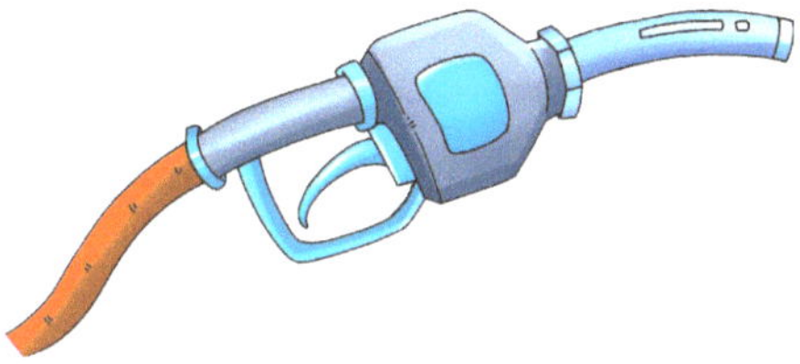

Handle ☐ Nozzle ☐ Machine ☐

Game ☐ Cards ☐ Puzzle ☐

Shine ☐ Dazzle ☐ Eyes ☐

Game ☐ Cards ☐ Frizzy ☐

Shine ☐ Dizzy ☐ Eyes ☐

R-Controlled Vowels

Read the following words. Notice how the vowels a, e, i, o and u are followed by the r sound. Can you hear the r sound?

Car

Bird

Corn

Tern

Nurse

Read the story. Circle the words in which the vowels are followed by r.

Barbara's Cake

Barbara is baking a cake for her younger sister, Bertha. It is a surprise birthday present for her.

Barbara has brought butter, castor sugar, flour, eggs and milk. She will use a whisk to stir and mix everything together. She will then pour the mixture into a baker's tray and put it in the oven.

Barbara is sure Bertha will love her cake.

Teaching Tips:

When an r follows the vowel, it controls the sound of the vowel. You can hear only the little bit of 'a' and more of 'r.' The silent e rule works well with vowels followed by r.

Word Bank.

Jar	Her	Fir	Torch	Fur
Yard	Clerk	Third	Chord	Burn
Large	Germ	Smirk	Stork	Purse
Lark	Nerve	Skirt	Thorn	Hurt

Sort the following words into the correct group.

Chirp	Mother	Farm	Purse
Horse	Fork	Tiger	Explore
Blurt	Horn	Father	Park
Dart	Church	Nurse	Turn
Corn	Barn	Star	Torch

| Ir | Er | Ar | Or | Ur |

Hard C and Soft C

Read the following words. Notice that in some words c sounds like an s and in some it sounds like kuh (k).

Cat

Cycle

Cup

Circle

Colt

Colour the hard c words blue and the soft c words orange in the story.

Cinderella at the Circus

One day, a circus came to the city. Cinderella, the princess, was very excited. She told the prince about it. The prince took Cinderella to the circus. They bought tickets and took the seats closest to the circle. The first act was a cat on a bicycle. Candy the clown came next. The prince noticed that the clown was crying. He told Cinderella about it. Cinderella asked Candy what was wrong. He told her that one of the children in the audience had beaten the cat. Cinderella took the cat to the vet. The vet gave it medicines. Soon, the cat was fine.

Teaching Tips:

The letter c can stand for a soft s sound or a hard kuh sound. When a c comes before e, i, y it sounds like s. This is called the soft c. If it's any other letter, the c sounds like kuh. This is called the hard c.

Word Bank.

Cap	Cymbal	Centre
Citizen	Curly	Comedy

Say the name of the picture aloud. Circle the words that begin with a hard c sound. Underline the words that begin with a soft c sound.

Clock	City	Car
Candy	Carrot	Circle
Camera	Coat	Celery

Hard G and Soft G

Read the following words. Notice that in some words, the g sound is hard like guh and in some it is soft and sounds like j.

Goat

Giant

Ginger

Goblin

Gerbil

Circle the soft g words and underline the hard g words in the story.

Geril and the Giant

There was a gentle giant who lived in a house with a big gate. He lived with a girl called Geril. Geril was as kind as the gentle giant. They sat in their garden amidst the green grass and enjoyed eating gems with ginger ale. The giant liked to gossip with Geril. Geril called her friends to play games in the garden. As people passed their gate, they said, 'Hello Geril and gentle Giant.'

Teaching Tips:

If the letter g is in front of the vowel a, o, or u, then it usually takes its own hard sound of g. If it is in front of the vowels e, i or y, then it sounds like j.

www.ingramcontent.com/pod-product-compliance
Lightning Source LLC
Chambersburg PA
CBHW040057160426
43192CB00002B/90